Touching

the
INVISIBLE

Living by Unseen Realities

Touching
the
INVISIBLE

Living by Unseen Realities

Norman Grubb

PUBLICATIONS

Fort Washington, PA 19034

Touching the Invisible

Published by CLC Publications

U.S.A.
P.O. Box 1449, Fort Washington, PA 19034

GREAT BRITAIN
51 The Dean, Alresford, Hants. SO24 9BJ

Printed in the United States of America

ISBN-13 (mass market) 978-0-87508-975-1
ISBN-13 (e-book) 978-1-61958-032-9

Contents

Page

Preface 7

1. The First Secret We Learned 11

2. The Key to Success 17

3. The Technique of Faith....................23

4. How to Obtain Guidance.................31

5. The Lie of the Ages........................39

6. The Adventure of Adversity 45

7. Almighty Meekness 51

8. How to Maintain Unity 63

9. The Key to a Released Personality......75

10. The Law of Spiritual Harvest............91

Preface

DURING our earlier years in the Worldwide Evangelization Crusade we were confronted with two problems which greatly occupied our attention, and the ensuing chapters give an outline of the answer to them, which remains today as much the right answer as then.

The first has been: is there an infallible secret of success in any piece of work undertaken under the guidance of God? We began to ask that question at a time of almost hopeless internal chaos and external difficulties. The practical details of how the answer was found, its many varied applications and the results that followed are to be found in various other publications of the crusade, but the general evidence is seen in the fact that the Mission which then had thirty-five workers in one field with one home base, has increased through the economic difficulties of those days, and through war years, until today there are the two crusades, the Worldwide Evangelization Crusade* and the Christian Literature Crusade**—the WEC with 950 workers in twenty-nine fields and ten sending bases, and the CLC with 350 workers in thirty-one fields. All this is attributable to the discovery and application of the one scriptural secret of success, which God has laid down for the guidance and use of His servants all through the pages of the Bible.

I have published several other books in an endeavor to give a thorough examination and exposition of this fundamental dynamic of all Christian living. These include *God Unlimited* and (the latest) *Who Am I?* But the chapters of this present little book give glimpses of the light revealed. These may not be found to be easy reading, and certainly they need more thorough exposition; but we know by experience that thousands of Christians are hungry today for the teaching and light which go to the root of

---

* Now WEC International (Worldwide Evangelization for Christ)

** Now CLC Ministries International

all problems of life and service, and we hope that these pages will at least open a window upon the hidden treasure.

The second problem has been: is there an infallible method of maintaining a healthy spirit of fellowship in a Christian organization? Sad experience had driven home to us the fact that the zeal and faith of a body of Christians often outruns the manifestation of fervent love in its own ranks. To this also an answer was found and put to the test of experience. Failures there have been, but as the years have passed the general standard of unity, mutual trust and family fellowship attained only confirms us in the certainty that the solution discussed in a chapter of this book gives the one law for the maintenance of Christian unity.

The proof that the light of God shines in some measure through these pages will be that it shines into our hearts as we read and sends us out more fitted to experience in our own spheres of service God's word to Joshua, "Then thou shalt make thy way prosperous, and then thou shalt have good success."

Norman P. Grubb
1976

1

The First Secret We Learned

WE have a daily meeting at our London headquarters. This does not sound either original or unique, for what Christian organization does not? But we are going to begin by describing its special characteristics for a particular reason. It is the methods we have been led to adopt in these meetings which have been the foundation of the advance of the crusade in times when the only normal course would have been to retrench or put up the shutters.[1]

Practically all can be traced to a great discovery. It had been our custom to divide our prayer meetings into two portions, one for reading the

---

1. The methods of carrying on the morning meetings vary somewhat, now that there are ten national headquarters and thirty-five fields; but the basic principles of operating by guidance and faith remain the same throughout the Crusade.

Scriptures, with a few general comments, and the other for open prayer. But much of the praying, although sincere, was without strong assurance, because so often we were not sure if our requests were according to God's will. Therefore, most requests would be prefaced by some such phrase as "If it is Thy will." Often we rose from our knees as uncertain in heart about the answer as before we asked, and if we had been questioned whether this or that prayer would be granted, we could only have said "We hope so."

We had, however, begun to observe another emphasis in the prayer lives of the men of the Bible. We saw that they went much farther back than we did. They first discovered whether their prayer was God's will; then, having received assurance on this point, they prayed, received by faith, persisted, declared things to come, with all the authority of God Himself. We saw this in countless cases. Elijah suddenly appears on the scene and announces, "As the Lord God of Israel liveth, there shall not be dew nor rain these years but according to my word"; and James tells us that this was "effectual praying." The contrast struck us between Hezekiah, a man of sincere but unavailing prayer, and Isaiah, a man of effectual prayer. In a crisis Hezekiah cries to God and sends to Isaiah to say, "This is a day of rebuke; for the children are come to the birth, and there is not strength to bring forth. *It may be* that the Lord will hear the words of Rabshakeh and will reprove. . . ." But Isaiah's answer is "Thus saith the Lord, Be not afraid . . . behold, *I will* send a blast upon him."

So it became more and more impressed on us that effectual praying must be guided praying: that the first essential was not to pray, but to know what to pray for. Special and clear provision has been made for this in the Scriptures, when Paul said in Romans 8:26–27 that the Spirit is given expressly to guide our praying, for true prayers are God's prayers prayed through us: they issue from God's mind, are taught us by His Spirit, are prayed in His faith, and are thus assured of answer. On this basis our meetings took a new form. Guidance must be found. We must go to our knees only when we know from God for what we are going. To obtain this, formality, time limits and human control must go.

The entire household gathers at 9:00 a.m.,

anything from twenty-five to forty of us. The objective of the meetings is entirely practical, not a study of doctrine nor a Bible reading, but the tackling of the immediate problems of the work. It may concern a number of new recruits for the fields and the need of finance for them; the granting of a government permit to open a new area of work; a tribe unyielded to the gospel; a difficulty between workers. The matter is outlined and discussed. Opinions and criticisms are invited. Gradually the conviction gains ground among us all that such and such an outcome would glorify God—a certain sum of money by a certain date; a move of the Spirit at a certain place; the granting of an official permit; a reconciliation. The Scriptures are then examined. What examples have we as a ground for our faith? We turn to David, Daniel, Moses, Paul. Were they sure of their guidance? Did they believe and declare it? Did it come to pass? Can we fairly compare our situation to theirs? If so, then—and only then—we pray, believe, receive, declare our faith and persist, with all the authority of the Master's words: "Whosoever shall *say*" (the word of command, much stronger than "pray") "unto this mountain, Be thou removed

. . . and shall not doubt in his heart, but shall believe that those things which he saith shall come to pass, he shall have whatsoever he saith."

2

The Key to Success

THE one word which has stood out pre-eminently before us these years has been "faith." We found full authority in the Scriptures for a strong emphasis upon it. Outstandingly is this so in Hebrews 11, where every life of notable achievement in the Bible is labeled with a single incisive phrase as its keynote: "By *faith.*" Christ, too, put remarkable emphasis on faith. To practically every miracle of healing He added a comment such as, "Thy faith hath saved thee"; "According to your faith be it unto you"; "If thou canst believe, all things are possible to him that believeth."

We remember how in our earlier days of Christian service we often wished to rewrite these statements. We thought that stress would be put in the more proper place if they were changed to "By the power of God" instead of "By faith"; and "The Lord hath saved thee" instead of "Thy faith hath saved thee." Now, however, we had begun to understand the whole point to be that the inflow of almighty power into Christian lives is potentially ceaseless and can be taken for granted through grace; but what is so rare and therefore necessary of emphasis is the faith that applies it.

All believers say in a general way, "God is Almighty," "God can do this or that." Only one in a thousand says, "God is almighty in *me*" and "God will do so and so through *me.*" Here lay the essence of Moses' controversy with God at the burning bush. God was saying, "Come now, I will send *thee,* and *thou* wilt deliver My people." Moses was replying, "I believe You can and will do it, but not through *me.*" God's almightiness was not the point in question. It was Moses' appropriation and obedience of faith that hung in the balance. Thus when Moses did set forth to carry out the commission, the Holy Spirit rightly says it was done "by faith." The same difference in the quality of believing makes the dividing line between Elijah and the other seven thousand true believers who had not bowed the knee to Baal, and yet who had so little influence on the lives of their generation that Elijah did not know of their existence.

If we trace our weakness in the exercise of authoritative faith to the source, we shall find that our spiritual vitality is sapped at the roots through failure to take a bold grasp of the truth of "Christ in you" sufficient to shatter the illusion and consequent weakening effects of a false sense of separation. We know God only at a distance. We know touches of His power and grace, visitations which come and go. We are sure about the past through trust in His atoning work, and of the future through the promise of eternal life. But we have only a variable consciousness of His daily presence with us.

The transforming truth is that of our inward fusion with Him. "He that is joined to the Lord is one spirit." Can anything describe actual union more realistically than that? We *have* His mind. We *have* His power. If all power is in Him, all power is in us. This was the transforming revelation to the men of faith of old. Moses had the call and the zeal as a young man, but at a critical moment he felt himself alone and fled. Forty years later he was baptized at the burning bush into realized union with the "I AM," and from that time spoke forth the word of authority and was unconquerable.

Armed with this realization—having pressed through by death and resurrection to an almost unconscious abiding in Christ—so natural does it become that we begin to live secretly with God in an invisible world whose resources become more real to us than the visible. Indeed, we see that the visible is only a local, temporal manifestation of the invisible, "the visible is made out of the invisible" (Heb. 11:3, Moffatt) and that therefore we are dwelling at the center and source of all things, whereas the Christian to whom the "material" is still the more real dwells mainly on the circumference.

When we are faced, for example, with financial need, fixed in God we are not moved. We say, "The outward silver and gold that we need is only His creation. We dwell with the Creator, and take our supply from Him as He has told us to do." *Are we to be such fools as to limit our plans for worldwide evangelization to our visible, immediate bank balance, when the treasury of the universe is ours?* To do this would be to walk in the flesh, not the Spirit. A thousand times over we have proved the reality of the invisible, as faith exercised and declared has become material substance.

3

The Technique of Faith

IN digging more deeply into this "law of faith" (Rom. 3:27), so that we might know and apply God's method in the performance of our God-appointed task, one of the revelations we found in the Scriptures was the way by which God Himself performed His own first task of creation. We were quick to realize that the same God indwelling us would use the same eternal principles in completing His new creation.

We found the key in the saying of John that all things were made by the Word—an expression of immense significance. Slaves as we are to the visible and tangible, we make much of deeds and little of words. Yet here we glimpse the truth that the *Word* of God is creative, and that "things" are merely the outcome of the Word, the effect that proceeds from the cause.

How striking, too, that modern science is

just awaking to this. For years people surmised that the ultimate form of matter was the atom— hard, round, indivisible particles like minute billiard balls. Not a scientist believes that today. Atoms have been resolved into neutrons and electrons, immaterial and infinitesimal charges of electricity. Endeavors to explain the structure of electrons can only be made by the most abstruse mathematical formulae. So far back, indeed, have investigations into the origin of matter now been pushed, that some scientists are beginning to admit that physics will never get there, for the roots lie in a spiritual and mental realm inaccessible to present-day science.

They glimpse what the Spirit revealed to John two thousand years ago, that matter comes from mind: that mind—first the thought, then the word, then the thing—is the divine and universal order for the manifestation of all that is. The Father, the Son and the Spirit: the blessed and eternal Trinity, each in the other, each proceeding from the other in His own order, each acting according to His function, is found to be the root and ground of all created things.

Once again that saying of John gives us our point. The Word, the Son, is begotten of the

Thought or Thinker, the Father. From the Word proceeds the creating Spirit. "Let there be light" was first in the mind of the Father. The thought, finding definition in the word, proceeded with creative authority from the mouth of the Son, outlining with exactitude each stage in the tremendous edifice of creation. The word took form by the Spirit, as He brooded over the dark waters. The Father thought it; the Son said it; the Spirit produced it: "And there was light." Here is the creative process of the Godhead.

To produce the new creation in Christ Jesus, the unchanging God could use only this one method, which is His own nature in action. The Father conceived the plan; the Son gave it definition by His incarnation, death and resurrection, and declared the creative word of authority "Come unto Me," "I am the Way"; the Spirit brings into being the new life in all who believe. Yet more important for our present purpose, however, is the realization that the Godhead who now indwells regenerate man, still works and can only work by this one unchangeable process. The Father thinks His thoughts in man. The Son speaks His creative word of faith by man. The Spirit manifests the substance through man. "It is God that dwelleth in us to will and to do of His good pleasure."

One responsibility lies with man—only one, but so pivotal that all the outcome is attributed to this one activity. Man must carry out the process of faith. Fallen but redeemed man has to arise and grasp the heights and depths of the fact that he is a son in Christ, together with the Son, and that he is now to cooperate with this recreative process of the Godhead.

At regeneration, by the mercy of God he "believes" almost mechanically; God's thoughts regarding sin are revealed to and in him; God's word of salvation, Jesus, is declared to him; God's creative work by the Spirit is wrought in him—all by his simple act of honest reception, his first elementary exploit of faith. But if he is to go on himself to be God's coworker, he has to be trained in the laws of the divine working. A knowledge of God's acts may suffice for the personal redemption of the children of Israel; but Moses, to be a redeemer as well as a recipient of redemption, must know God's ways (Ps. 103:7). It is the difference in usefulness between the passenger and the driver of a car.

God's servant has to learn not merely how

faith gives entrance into the heavenly life, but also how faith maintains as a reality the indissoluble union between man's regenerate spirit and God's Spirit, that region of abiding in a simple, single-eyed, pure-hearted relationship where God's thoughts are inwardly revealed, Christ's word of authority spoken through human lips, and the Spirit's mighty works manifested before all the world. The thought of faith is expressed in the word of faith, resulting in the substance of faith.

As we then applied these truths to our own situations, the first essential was obvious. God is to think His thoughts in us. The apostle's saying that "We have the mind of Christ" (1 Cor. 2:16) is to be a reality. Many ask, "Is it possible to know God's will confidently in all situations?" It is. We have already described the method of our meetings—resulting maybe immediately, maybe after days or weeks, in an inward certainty: clear, peaceful, indescribable— that "such and such is God's will in this thing." Before this comes, we never move, never pray, unless it be merely for light; but we can now arise and advance. The first stage is completed. God has made known His mind.

Now the word of faith must be brought into action. Is it not at this point that God's people constantly fail? Was not every one of the men of God in the Scriptures characterized first by being a man who had inward movings and assurances of the Spirit, and then by outspoken declarations of a "Thus saith the Lord"—the word of faith which was the outcome of interior guidance? For it is the word of the Lord, as the necessary outbirth from the thought of the Lord, which the Scripture testifies to be almighty.

Why do we stop short of this? Because we are still so carnal. "O ye of little faith." "O faithless generation, how long shall I be with you and suffer you?" Carnality is to be under the influence of the visible, tangible and temporal, instead of the invisible, intangible, eternal. We fail to bridge the gap within us between God's thoughts and God's word of faith because we are bound by the domination of the visible. We see the blind eye, the withered arm: Christ saw the will and power of His Father to heal, and spoke the word, "Stretch forth thine arm," "Receive thy sight." We see the five loaves and the multitudes, and say, "What are they among so many?" Christ saw His Father's invisible and unlimited supply, gave thanks for it, acted on the full assurance of it, and faith was seen to be "the giving of substance to things hoped for."

We have learned in the WEC that we have one great enemy of faith—within us, and not in our circumstances—fear of the visible. We know the inward urges of the mind of God to some certain end. We know the next step: not to ask for faith, but to exercise it (Why ask for what we already have? If the author and finisher of faith is within us, all faith is there already for the using). We must declare that what we desire (His desire in us) will come to pass—add the word of faith to the thought of faith. Then the battle is joined. The fear of some visible giant paralyzes us. An opposing government, the need of funds, the hardness of a fanatical people, the grip of an illusion: the vision of the flesh lusts against the vision of the Spirit.

In Jesus' name we break through. We declare the word of faith, "That government will give way," "That area will be opened," "That money will come," "Those souls will be saved." The word, if we are rightly abiding, is spoken in the same power and through the same Person who made the declaration at the earliest dawn of history, "Let there be light." It is repeated again and again as occasion arises—not prayer, nor aspiration, nor hope; but praise, declaration, quiet reception of a supply already given, a calling of those things that be not as though they were. As we do that, the manifestation of the thing believed comes to pass as surely as the harvest follows the sowing.

God's thought. God's word of faith. God's substance. That is God's order in Himself at the creation, and in us as His instruments of the new creation.

4

How to Obtain Guidance

FROM what has already been said concerning the way of faith, the question will certainly have arisen in the mind: But how can I know God's will? Indeed there is hardly any question that is more frequently asked than this. The reason is obvious from what has gone before. Until we know God's voice and how to hear Him speaking, we are conscious of instability in our Christian service. In multitudes of cases our difficulty is not unwillingness to go here, do this, or say that, but uncertainty as to whether God is telling us so to act. The lack in our prayer life is not so much a lack of zeal, or failure to ask, but a lack of faith and assurance in asking, derived from uncertainty as to God's will. "We know not what to pray for as we ought."

Now the opposite is manifest in the Scriptures. The keynote to every great life there described is that they merely did what God told them to do. "The Lord said unto Moses." Paul "heard a voice saying unto him." And supremely, Christ said, "The words that I speak I speak not of Myself: but the Father that dwelleth in Me, He doeth the works."

Now this last saying of Christ is of great importance, for it does away with an idea I mistakenly held for some years, which is also held by many others. I used to say, "If only God would speak to me in an audible voice or vision, as to the men of the Bible, I would know how to act." But Christ here says that He was guided by an indwelling voice, not an external appearance; and I discovered that in the great majority of instances in Bible history the same is true, for we have no right to imagine an audible voice or visible appearance, unless it is distinctly stated to be such.

This important fact brings guidance within my reach and that of all believers. Visions and voices are extremely rare, indeed unknown in the experience of the writer, though we have no right to limit God in His manner of revelation; but communion with an indwelling Person is the privilege of all and the unceasing experience of some.

Another point to be noted is that guidance is the direct communication of the Spirit with our spirits and is not to be confused with the Scriptures. God's written word is the general guide to His people. The Bible is the inspired and infallible revelation of the principles of Christian living, and any individual guidance which does not conform to it is from a false source. Also in some cases a sentence of Scripture may be the medium by which the Spirit speaks to us. Even then the point that makes it guidance to me is its application *by the Spirit* to a given situation—its leaping, as it were, out of the book into my heart. *The Spirit* gives the guidance. It is always in conformity with the Scriptures, and may be in the words of Scripture, but it is the indwelling Spirit who guides. Romans 8:16 gives us the primary instance of spiritual communion in every believer's life, the Spirit bearing witness with our spirit. Guidance, then, as to the details of living is only an extension of the inner speaking and hearing established through the blood of reconciliation and recognition of the indwelling Spirit.

Realizing, then, that guidance is to be obtained from an indwelling Person, the Holy

Spirit, and is the privilege of all believers, we will examine the manner of obtaining it. The best way known to the writer—and one practised continually in our daily headquarter meetings when dealing with our crusade problems—is as follows: First, we make as sure as possible that we approach the subject upon which we desire light as God's servants seeking the fulfillment of His will in His way; this, of course, should not and does not take long, for it is the normal attitude of Christ-indwelt lives. We examine ourselves to make as certain as we can that our objective is His glory, and that we are ready to do all that He may say.

Then we recognize and utilize the mind in its rightful position. It is at this point that there is most confusion in the matter of guidance. Some put too much emphasis on the human reason, "common sense," confusing it with the Lord's voice: others too little, turning from it as from a carnal thing and attempting to find guidance with an emptied mind. The truth is that the human reason is a preeminently useful servant but was never created to be the final arbiter of truth in the human personality. The exaltation of the human reason to the throne of authority in life is the sin of "the wise of this world."

The reason is the great sorting house, but not the sorter. Its function is to investigate, tabulate, theorize, memorize, but not to direct. That is the function of the Spirit in the regenerated life. Sanctified reason remains the noble endowment by which man can contemplate and expound the heights and depths of the divine mysteries; but direction leading to decision is to be found in the renewed spirit, the dwelling place and throne room of the Holy Spirit. Thus the man who knew guidance more perfectly than any other in Bible days, Moses, makes the clear distinction, when he said concerning the source of his authoritative declarations, "Hereby ye shall know that the Lord hath sent me to do all these works; for I have not done them of my own mind" (Num. 16:28). His reasoning and expository faculties were the instrument for the reception and declaration of God's revelations. The reason is to be used to the full, but not abused: it is to be the instrument of guidance, but not the guide.

Consonant with this, we thoughtfully examine our situation, know all that we can about it, let the Scripture throw any light upon it, but then we refuse by such reasonings and investigations to make the decision. That must come from the inner witness.

So, in order to know His voice, we now change our tactics. We have been occupied in thinking over our problem, but now we deliberately cease to think about it. When God speaks, He always speaks in stillness. While our hearts are disturbed and our minds busy on a situation, His voice cannot be heard. Our inward attitude must be like a pool of water. If disturbed, no reflection can be seen in it. When still, the features can be seen. So the best thing we can do, having stored our mind with the facts, is to leave them with God. It is not a state of forgetfulness but a redirection of our attention. We were concentrated on the problem; now we concentrate on Him, the solver.

We do not attempt to strain for an answer, nor to make one up. We remain like little children, free from concern, free from urge, but refusing to act until we know. We maintain that we have a right to know, for by His grace we are His servants and the one thing to which a servant has a right is orders.

Then the conviction comes. It does not matter how it comes, so long as it comes. Often circumstances arrange themselves so as to make a certain course obvious—this is a very usual occurrence. Sometimes a verse of Scripture or a strong inner assurance is the way. But the point is that whatever means the Spirit uses, He communicates to our spirits, through a mind stored with the facts, a solid certainty that thus and thus is God's way. That is the peace of God sitting as a referee (Col. 3:15), and declaring God's verdict on the situation. When we know that, then we can act, declare, believe, in full assurance of faith; for we go out, not to gain a victory or find a way, but to gather the spoils of a victory already won, or to reach a goal with the map of directions already in our hands.

5

The Lie of the Ages

IN a previous chapter we have stressed "false separation" as the source of the weakness of God's people. Man was not made to be separate from God, nor indeed from his fellow man. Preeminently, he was created spirit to be in union and communion with the Spirit, expressing forth the powers and glories of that inner united life through soul (personality) and body. As created spirit, he was also to be in like union and communion with other created spirits, his brethren, as with the Father of spirits.

The Fall cut the cable. Sin, the fruit of selfishness, broke the union between man's spirit and the Holy Spirit. Man became a unitary self, fighting for his own ends against other selves, and alienated from the Father of selves, God, who is love, the bond of perfectness. The sense of separation replaced the sense of union, and man was henceforward shut in to the puny powers of his individual resources of mind and body impregnated by the spirit of disobedience.

The Redeemer came, God manifest in the flesh, and made atonement by His outpoured life. He completed the work, taking into His death the all of sin, root and fruit, the self-attitude and its consequent criminal acts

(He bore our sins, 1 Pet. 2:24; He was made sin, 2 Cor. 5:21). Thus He opened the door for all believers to much more than just pardon and reconciliation. It was to our lost heritage of *reunion* that He restored us.

It was for the destruction of the reality and sense of separation from God, which is the cause of our weakness, that He died. He symbolized this for us by such examples as the vine and branches—for these are inseparable, one life, one organism. The Holy Ghost through Paul used the further illustration of head and body, which cannot be conceived of as apart. Direct expressions brought home the same truth—such as "Christ our life," "Not I, but Christ liveth in me," "Christ is all and in all." The strongest language that could be used was used to delineate spiritual union and unity.

Just here lies the error of God's people, and
the deceit of Satan. He will make it always appear to us that there is still this old separation,
the fruit of the Fall. God is still away there in
heaven, while we are here on earth; whereas
the Scripture says that, even with regard to the
risen and ascended Christ, we are raised and
seated with Him—in Him in the heavenlies,
even as He is in us in the earthlies, a spiritual
union beyond adequate description by human
language. Satan knows that if he can keep us in
the delusion of separation, we are at his mercy,
weak in a crisis, wavering in a decision. We feel
our weakness, bewail our ignorance, for we see
our separate selves and know their limitations
and corruptions; and the best we can attain to is
to call on God to send help from without, and
struggle to believe that He will.

If we cast aside the suggestions of Satan, the
delusions of our own feelings of separation, the
sense of weakness and ignorance; if we boldly
possess our possessions in Christ, draw the
sword of the Spirit upon the deceiver, declare
by God's word that we are one with Christ and
with one another, one mystic organism, one
divine life flowing in and through all—then we

are strong by faith, for His strength is in us; we *are* wise, for His wisdom is ours; we *have* love, joy, or any other needed grace of the Spirit, for we are permeated with Him. All we need to do is to go forward in this faith, as having and possessing, and we shall find that what is true in the realm of the Spirit becomes manifest in the realm of the senses, whether it be power, love, joy, knowledge, or any other needed resource. Christ the head thus becomes manifest in and through His members.

On this basis we can understand the reason for Christ's drastic statements concerning earthly and personal attachments—if we do not hate loved ones, possessions, life itself, we cannot be His disciples. For, to enter into realized possession of universal love, resources, and life in God, there has to be a dying out to the personal, human, and thus narrowing earthly attachments. Does this mean loss? When Christ "lost" the glory of His Godhead and took the form of a servant, when He "lost" His earthly home, parents, property and life to found a world family, did He lose? When prophets and apostles of old, martyrs and missionaries of recent centuries, "lost" all to bring men to God, did they lose?

When C.T. Studd "lost" earthly fame, fortune, home, to found a worldwide crusade, did he lose? Nor did such surrender of earthly attachments mean loss of true love or failure to fulfill responsibilities to earthly loved ones. Rather, it means a purifying love towards them, a love which, enlarged in capacity to a whole world, becomes at the same time increased in depth and tenderness to every individual. May we see the gain, not loss, and press up this narrow path by faith and obedience to realized union with God which alone is abundant and eternal life.

6

The Adventure of Adversity

A NOTHER of the great principles of victorious Christian service which God has been teaching us in our headquarter meetings is the true method of facing, handling and using for good all forms of adversity, all experiences of what we call evil—shocks, suffering, difficulty, disasters, unjust treatments.

The first key, put in a sentence, has been this: that our "evils" are never the happenings in themselves, but the effect we allow them to have on us. No matter whether objectively an experience is apparently good or evil, subjectively, to the one who fears and doubts, all is evil; to the one who trusts, all is good.

The supreme example of this is Calvary. At Gethsemane, at the entrance to the darkest valley ever trodden by man, the Savior faced the most devilish of outward experiences, but dissolved their evil effects upon Himself by an inward attitude of faith which declared them to be good. He rejected the temptation to regard them as evil when He said, "Not My will." He declared all that was coming to be inherently good when He said, "Thy will be done." His predominant thoughts and words during His last hours with His disciples were of fullness of joy, of cheerfulness, of a peace unknown to the world, of glory present and future. When the author of evil was mentioned, He dismissed him with the mere passing reference, "The prince of this world cometh, and hath nothing in Me." Note the preposition "in." Satan could make a fierce enough attack upon His outward frame, but faith made it impossible for him to touch the true man within. To all appearances Calvary was totally evil, and the Scriptures themselves say that Calvary was Satan-engineered; but Peter later confirmed his Master's attitude, by the inspiration of the Holy Ghost, when he declared that He had been delivered unto death "by the determinate counsel and foreknowledge of God." So then the believer also can say, "All that happens to me, no matter how evil in itself, I declare as good to me, and nothing evil."

But the adventure of adversity goes deeper than this. When seen in its true perspective, it is found to be the doorway into God's most transcendent secret—that adversities and sufferings, which in their origin are the effects of sin and instruments of the devil, in the grasp of faith become *redemptive*. They are transfigured from the realm of merely something to be endured as an opposition of Satan, to something to be used to conquer their author and redeem his victims. Faith in time of adversity makes the serpent swallow itself! Once again the supreme proof of this is that when Satan made his fiercest attack in history on the person of Christ, God used that attack, through the faith and endurance of the Sufferer, to bring about the world's salvation. *God uses evil to bring about good*—not causing it, but using it.

The consequence of a clear grasp of this fact, that Satan and all evil circumstances in our lives are God's most useful instruments for the fulfillment of His purposes, is obvious. All attacks of Satan are seen to be our blessings. We "count them all joy." We "rejoice in tribulation." We use them as special opportunities to see the manifestation of God's power, instead of merely enduring them with a struggle as "judgments" or "tests." This truth, indeed, transmutes into strength one of the weakest joints in the armor of God's people, a tendency to look upon trials and adversities merely as means by which God satisfies Himself as to our fidelity; instead of realizing that sufferings are the fulfillment of an inevitable law in the working out of God's purposes, and that the most highly honored and trusted of His servants are those who are counted worthy to "fill up that which is behind [lacking] of the afflictions of Christ *for His body's sake*" (Col. 1:24).

The truth is that by no other way than by Christ's sufferings could a fallen world return to God. In the first Adam and his seed there was a dying to God and a rising to sin. In the last Adam and His seed there must be a dying to sin and a rising to God. Christ the captain of our salvation was made perfect as a Savior through sufferings. Faith transformed the contradiction of sinners into the means of their salvation. We follow in His steps, not to gain our salvation (which is His free gift), but by transmuting our trials into victories of faith we cooperate with the Great Victor in bringing His victory to a defeated and enslaved world.

Thus to Christ's followers, who glimpse the glorious purpose and triumph in and through evils and sufferings, the acceptance and endurance of them becomes an adventure of faith. Thus and thus alone does the Christian warrior laugh the laugh of faith. If God's gifts are our blessings, and the devil's assaults are also our blessings, what remains to harm or depress us? If good is good, and evil is equally good to the enlightened, then a realm of life is entered where we rejoice always, in everything give thanks, and in all things are more than conquerors.

7

Almighty Meekness

THERE is the work of the cross and there is the way of the cross. All believers accept the former. "Upon Another's life, Another's death, I rest my whole eternity." But much slower are we to recognize that the cross represents not merely the atoning act, but also an eternal principle, a fundamental of the nature of God, underlying the act—that the atonement, the work of the cross, has as its objective the recall of mankind to this fundamental principle, this way of the cross, this nature of the Godhead, a way so revolutionary that it cuts at the root of man's recognized method of actions from primitive savagedom to modern civilization.

Two rival principles of action joined battle at Calvary, and call the world's attention to their relative claims—force versus meekness.

The way of force the world has known and

practiced from its infancy. Force gained its kingdom by usurpation at the Fall, and publicly proclaimed its dominion over the affairs of men by the side of the slain body of Abel. At that critical moment God stepped in. In order to prevent lawlessness and violence from bringing total disaster on the infant race, God instructed man in the rule of law. He taught him how to subdue force by force, and laid down in those early days the groundwork of the legal system which now governs civilization, instructing Noah that "whoso sheddeth man's blood, by man shall his blood be shed," giving Israel, as a standard of strict justice, "an eye for an eye and a tooth for a tooth." Right on into New Testament days and up to our present era these safeguards to a just and ordered social and international life have been approved and maintained, Paul saying that "the powers that be are ordained of God," and that the magistrate "beareth not the sword in vain," law courts, police, jails and defense forces being the modern counterparts of this age-long system.

Yet two thousand years ago the world was introduced to another kingdom, based on other sanctions. In this realm the inheritors of the earth are said to be the meek, not the grasping and violent; giving, not getting, is the means of prosperity; wrongful activities are overcome by a counterattack of good deeds; enemies are loved, blessed, kindly entreated, not hated. Indeed, its Founder distinctly states that its principles supersede those of the era of law. "It hath been said by them of old time," said He, "but I say unto you . . ." And what He verbally enunciated as a principle, later He acted out to the utmost limits when urged to oppose by violence His impending doom, answering, "My kingdom is not of this world: if My kingdom were of this world, then would My servants fight." From that day onward for all time the cross has become the symbol to the human race of a new, unknown, unguessed power, the unconquerable potency of defenseless, quenchless love.

> 'Twas on a day of rout they girded Me about
> They wounded all My brow, and they smote
> Me through the side;
> My hand held no sword when I met their armèd
> horde,
> And the conqueror fell down, and the Conquered
> bruised his pride.
> What is this, unheard before, that the Unarmed
> make war,

And the Slain hath the gain, and the victor hath
the rout?

Granted this as an ultimate ideal, granted
that all men of faith look with assurance to the
yet distant day when unarmed love will rule over
the melted and transformed hearts of all men,
when even among the animal creation "the wolf
will lie down with the lamb," when the King of
love will lead His loving subjects like a shepherd:
but in the interim, what? Can wicked men and
wicked systems now be restrained by meekness
and love? It is a question that exercises the conscience of many believers.

The answer according to the Scriptures, so
far as the writer sees it, is that the reign of law
based on force will last as long as this dispensa-
tion lasts: it is God's provision for the restraint of
evil "that we may live a quiet and peaceable life
in all godliness," and has His blessing. But it is
only His permissive will, introduced into fallen
man's economy to save the race from destruction
after it had chosen the way of disobedience. What
was said by Christ concerning one provision of
that law, "Moses because of the hardness of your
hearts suffered you . . . : but from the beginning
it was not so," is applicable to the whole.

God's true nature, true method of government was revealed in Jesus, the love that produces a corresponding love which fulfills all law, the self-giving that inspires a like devoted self-giving in its creatures of all levels of life. He founded, by His outpoured life and infused Spirit, the true kingdom of God—at first in the hearts of His inner circle of followers, to be extended one day to the whole world. In accordance with the very nature of that kingdom, He does not force its full implications upon His subjects in this twilight era of mingled good and evil, when at best we only "see through a glass darkly." He merely revealed the full standards by lip and life, and when they entailed a peculiarly high standard of allegiance, He would quietly add, "He that is able to receive it, let him receive it," or "If thou wilt be perfect," do such and such.

Gradually, as the centuries have passed, these seed thoughts have germinated and produced fruits, first only in scattered individuals and groups, usually regarded as dangerous maniacs by established "Christianity," and often per-secuted; then later, through their witness and often martyrdom, the higher light has reached the general conscience of humanity. Thus polygamy, allowed in Old Testament days, nowhere condemned in downright terms in the New Testament, became universally recognized as a sin and outlawed. Slavery has followed. The old imperialism, the subjugation of one race for the benefit of another, has in our generation begun to be recognized as immoral and un-Christian, to be followed soon by the full realization that God "hath made of one blood all nations of men," and that therefore all national barriers producing national prejudices, pride, enmities, selfishness are equally un-Christian. Religious persecution, when compared to the attitude of the Church of the Middle Ages, is now coming under universal condemnation. Inequality of privilege, class distinctions, unequal distribution of wealth, are now actively disturbing the conscience of mankind. Equally the cry is going up for the outlawing of war as a method for the settlement of national differences.

In the van of this "pacifist" movement, so far as war is concerned, come once again the "extremists," but already there are the thousands of today in place of the mere handful in the Great War twenty years ago, who feel it un-Christian to use weapons of destruction, defensive as well as offensive. Such "conscientiously object" to taking part in war. So few were they in 1914 and so fanatical in the eyes of their fellow Christians, that even in "Christian" England they were imprisoned and treated as criminals. Today in this 1939 war their viewpoint carries sufficient weight in Britain for tribunals to be set up to examine each case and exempt the sincere, although in most other countries the penalty for "pacifism" is still the broad arrow.

To our mind their stand for total meekness as a principle of the kingdom of God is in conformity with the full stature of Christ. All through Christian history enlightened groups have held fast to it. They have been and still are the forerunners and pioneers of the new age which will only dawn in fullness when its founder and first pioneer Himself appears to reign on earth. Meanwhile, it is "given" to some to see and follow thus literally in their Master's footsteps, and to them it is also given to bear witness to their conviction before the world.

Meekness unadulterated carries with it crucifixion. The truly meek can claim no rights, keep no rigid hold on earthly possessions. Not for them is recourse to the law courts or police.

Yet even now the meek inherit the earth. Many a missionary has found the almightiness of meekness—sometimes a woman alone, defenseless, possessionless amongst savages whom a government cannot subdue, yet finds that in a few years those raw barbarians are her devoted servants.

Contrast the use of force and meekness, and what do we find? Force is power on the circumference, meekness power at the center. Force is power on the outward and local, meekness is power on the inward and universal. Force is power visible, meekness power invisible. Force is man's human spirit putting forth its little energies, mental, verbal, physical, to attain its end. Meekness is God's Spirit, reigning in a man who first dies to all self attitudes and activities, and working through that man by His ways of love, faith, lowliness and long-suffering, the almighty works of God in that particular situation. Force *appears* strong. Meekness *appears* weak, but it is the weakness of God which is stronger than men, and the foolishness of God which is wiser than men.

Who won at Calvary, and is still winning and will win? The outward might of deep-laid scheme, mob violence and Roman law, or the inward, hidden might of the Lamb who opened not His mouth? Which have been more powerful, the legions of Caesar or the gospel of Jesus? Which convinces even an unregenerate world today as being the final truth, dictatorial compulsion or the Sermon on the Mount?

God's final word, fullness of wisdom and brightness of His glory, illuminated the world in the person of His Son. Christ brought to light by word and action this new way of conquest, this new method of government, this new dynamic power which swallows up the old way of force, unconquerable, eternal, irresistible—for it is the very nature of the Creator-Redeemer God in action. It is the way of the Lamb who opened not His mouth when led to the slaughter, and yet sits, still a Lamb, upon the throne of the universe. It is the way of One who is "meek and lowly in heart," the servant, the sufferer, and yet is given a name above every name at which every knee shall bow.

But, granted that we see this to be the way of Christ, how put it into action? First, there must be a conviction with us that meekness *is* power. Most folk regard meekness as a beautiful but negative Christian characteristic, an inert

yielding to circumstances or people too strong
for it, rather than as a positive spiritual weapon,
an almighty power. We have already outlined our
reasons for seeing it to be the latter.

Having settled that, the central core of meekness is that in every situation which arises we
must be sure that we die. Things occur which
move us to fear, anger, retaliation, argument,
self-defense. Under such impulses we leap to
the use of "force" by word or deed, whether only
in its mildest forms of urging our own view or
pursuing our own course of action. To all these,
in every such crisis, whether major or minor, we
must acquire the habit of dying and knowing
by the Spirit's witness that we have died. Such
a habit will be inwrought by the Spirit in the
experience of all who persistently take this way.

With that accomplished, we are lifted auto-
matically into "the heavenly places" of meekness.
A clear vision shows what would be the outcome
that honors God. An inborn faith gives assurance that it will come to pass, and a consequent
poise—the faith that overcomes the world. If we
speak, it is with the humility and tenderness of
Christ, with healing, not hurting, words. If we
act, it is in loving service. If we think or speak

of others, it is believing all things and hoping all things. Inward victory has been won. Inward power is flowing out. Outward circumstances and people will be conformed to that inward vision and faith. True "force" has won the day.

8

How to Maintain Unity

NO one can be long in a Christian organization without being brought face to face with the necessity that, in a community of God's servants, the personal zeal and faith of its members must be accompanied by the ability to live together in harmony. The key to fellowship is seen to be the next most important acquirement to holy living and love for souls. It must be admitted that among Christian communities of every type, holding every varied emphasis of Scriptural truth, zeal and knowledge far, far outrun the graces of dwelling together in unity, forbearing one another in love, and thinking no evil.

We ourselves were driven to this conviction some years back by our own failures, and what God has taught us on this subject we have had ample opportunity of putting to the proof these past nine years in the rapid growth of our numbers from forty to two hundred and twenty, and of our fields from one to eleven. There has been room enough for dissensions and division, nor have we been wholly free from them in individual instances and in one case on a young field; but on the whole we can only marvel at the heart-to-heart unity existing today between all fields and home bases, and between the workers on each field—which has made us only more sure that these principles of fellowship learned from God's Word are true.

What then are they? First we must make this clear. Unity is not the first fundamental. Unity is the lubricant essential to the operation of the machine; yet it is neither the machinery nor the motive power. First, therefore, we must be sure of our engine before we consider its lubrication. Therefore, when we speak here of unity we do not mean a unity without a doctrinal foundation, nor a unity which is made an end in itself, with any sort of compromise to attain it; we mean the uniting of a section of God's people based upon the common faith once delivered to the saints, and in our case with the common objective of worldwide evangelization.

So now to tackle our problem upon this understanding. We are a Christian organization, one in doctrine and one in general working methods. Within these limits unity is essential, yet 75 percent of our problems and calamities center around our failure to unite! What are the causes of disunity? *In the vast majority of cases they are the effect that the actions or attitude of a fellow worker have on us.* A coldness or neglect towards us is observed and felt, some habit or mannerism jars us, some apparently unspiritual behavior or method of work meets with our disapproval. Now there may well be real justification for this feeling, our judgment may be true, there may be real cause for concern. But here lies the secret. Christ gave it. He said words to this effect: "When you are tempted to criticize or resent, turn your attention to yourself and leave your brother alone." Recognize the beam of resentment and criticism in yourself; let the Holy Spirit deal with that, then you will be fitted to deal with your brother's mote. For either you will cease to notice it and it will be swallowed up in your renewed vision of all there is of Christ in him, or you will recognize that your Lord, who tenderly removes your faults in His own way, is also his Lord, who will do the same for him without your interference. Or, if in a rare case you are led to speak, it will be more a word of confession of your resentment than rebuke for his failure.

In other words, the first great secret of maintaining unity is—the moment I am inclined to criticize or resent a brother, I must recognize my spirit of criticism as the sin which concerns me, and not my brother's behavior: and I must keep on letting God deal with it till a spirit of appreciative love replaces it, by which I honor my brother instead of judging him, and rejoice in all of the image of Christ to be seen in him.

This is the outworking of what we often call "the victory of Calvary." Even in problems of relationships the way to life is through death, not only in ourselves but in others; for on such occasions as these, when we make it our occupation to see that we abide in Christ's death, the resurrection outcome is not merely the triumph of the spirit of love in our own hearts, but also the conquest of Christ in our brother's lives. We find ourselves empowered to claim the disappearance of the offending characteristic (if it is truly an offending thing); with ease we have assurance

that God is doing it, and in due course we see
the triumph of this miracle-working way of the
cross, this inheritance of the meek—for the
offending thing disappears and is replaced by
the graces of the Spirit, without the strain and
distress of painful conflicts, bitterness of spirit,
and often wrecked nerves and actual division.

From another angle we may say that the key
to the maintenance of happy and easy relationships between coworkers is the same that unlocks
the door to all our problems—*faith*, but this
time towards man. The immediate problem then
arises: how can we trust fallible men or they us?
We can love them—but how trust them? The
solution to this problem is that we are to act
towards our brethren as we do to ourselves. We
do not trust ourselves, but we do trust Christ in
us (Gal. 2:20); and as for ourselves apart from
Him, although recognizing our many faults and
fallibilities, we are quick to side with God in His
long-suffering of us, and to comfort ourselves
with the knowledge that He judges by the honest
motive rather than the poor production!

Now let us go further and apply to the other
members of the body what we have applied to
ourselves. Recognize Christ in them: count on

Christ in them. In so far as there is another nature observable in them, show them the same tolerance and sympathy as we do to ourselves. Believe that Christ is working Romans 6:11 out in them also, and that they are cooperating with Him. Reckon on the earnestness and sincerity of their discipleship, as much as we desire them to reckon on ours. By so doing we are effecting more than the maintenance of unity; by our faith we are building up our brethren in Christ, for, as we have already seen, faith is creative—just as conversely by our mistrust we help to pull down Christ's edifice in them.

For the maintenance of unity, therefore, we have only to look in the same direction as for the solution of all other problems: not to the solving of a problem without us, in our brethren or circumstances, but within our own selves.

There is an outlook on all men and things, proceeding from an inward condition, which radiates both inward and outward harmony. It is found in Paul's remarkable statement, "To the pure all things are pure"—an inward attitude of purity which sees all the contrasting evil and good of life not as a mixture, but as pure! Its effects are given us by the Lord Jesus when He says that singleness of eye (purity of eye proceeding from purity of heart) results in fullness of inward light, and therefore of peace and harmony, radiating out, of course, to all around.

How can we have this single eye, this purity in the effect of all things upon us, in a world of wickedness? The answer, as indicated, is to be found within. Science tells us that in the ordinary things of life, from the multitude of sights and sounds and contacts conveyed to us through our senses, our minds only actually select and retain a fragment of all the vibrations which pour in upon us, and that fragment accords with our mental outlook—so what we hear and feel is largely what we are within. Thus in seeing and describing a tree, for instance, the mind of a botanist will select and accept visible, tangible or oral impulses which conform to his outlook—points which concern the genealogy and life of the tree. The artist, on the other hand, will be enraptured with points which concern its form and coloring; the woodsman with its value for the sawmill; and so on. The condition of the mind is seen to control the choice of information conveyed through the senses, and to give a description and pass a judgment accordingly.

Follow out this line of thought in the things of the Spirit, and it will be seen to illuminate those sayings of Christ and Paul. The Christ-filled man will recognize the hidden perfections and purposes of the Creator and Redeemer working in and through all things, evil and good, and will fix his "pure eye" on that. The One who originally made all things "good" is still at work in all to consummate His final stated purpose: to "gather together in one all things in Christ," and upon this the "single eye" is fixed. On this basis, so far as his brethren are concerned, that individual will recognize and respond to all that is Christlike in them from among the multitude of information conveyed to him concerning them through his senses. There are devilish things in all abundance and reality, but the pure heart and eyes see the pure things—as it is said of God Himself, "Thou art of purer eyes than to behold evil." The two alternatives always present themselves to us: we can see at a glance the human or carnal in our brethren, or we can see the outlines of Christ. Because we ourselves have so much of the old graveclothes still clinging to us, we are quick to see those same characteristics in others; we can dwell on these and point them out, and thus foster disunity and distrust, as well as leanness to our own souls. On the other hand we can recognize in our brethren the divine image which has also been formed through grace in ourselves; we can rejoice in this, make it the subject of our comments, and thus foster unity, confidence, as well as fatness to our own souls. Along this line we can also see the weight of those other statements concerning criticism such as "Wherein thou judgest another thou condemnest thyself; for thou that judgest doest the same things"; and "With what judgment ye judge, ye shall be judged."

How greatly indeed we need the new mind in Christ concerning our brethren. The curse of the Fall has been to bring separation both from God and our neighbor. The center of our consciousness has been occupied with our separate selves. We have lost that instinctive spiritual union which was meant to be the original status of man: union with God and union with our fellow man, thus making, as it were, one supreme self of which we are each members, in place of a multitude of separate selves. This spiritual union is restored to us in Christ, in whom we are members of one body, members of one another: we in Him, He in us; and thus we may say we in each other. As our eyes open to this, we slowly learn that when we damage a brother we damage ourselves; and when we do good to a brother, we do good to ourselves. Thus Christ said, "Love your neighbor as yourself."

Even in dealing with the unsaved, in whom we cannot look for the image of Christ, there is an approach of love and trust which wins, while condemnation and castigation of sin often repels. The Lord Jesus was a magnet to sinners. Why? We learn the secret in the answer He gave the Pharisees in Luke 15, when they criticized His consorting with sinners. He revealed by the parables that followed that His attitude to the sinner was to regard him as a prodigal *son* and a lost *sheep.* Prodigal certainly, but also a son; lost, but also a sheep. Such words, quoted out of their context, could easily be misconstrued; but other passages make it clear beyond question that the sinner is lost eternally if he does not return to God. But from the point of view of the Shepherd and Savior seeking the wanderers, while not belittling that awful fact, the Christ-filled man also loves to remember that the sinner is "God's offspring," "lives, moves, and has his being in Him" (Acts 17:28), bears His image in a multitude of natural endowments, and above all has in him the light that enlightens all men (John 1:9)—which might be described as the unceasing inward movings of the Holy Spirit in preparation for conviction and conversion. This is a hidden work of grace which, despite the enmities and opposition of the fallen nature, engenders in all who are not absolute Christ-rejectors a response to the message of God's love, a longing for man's lost birthright of purity and power, and a disgust of a life spent among the swine. All great soul-winners know that it is this attitude of tenderness and confidence in man's readiness to hear and ability to respond which wins the day with the sinner. Thus once again, as with saint so with sinner, the golden key is faith.

9

The Key to a Released Personality

THE Spirit-filled life is presented to us by many different teachers from many different angles, each of which in our view makes its own contribution to the building of the "perfect man" in Christ. In our talks at our headquarter morning meetings we have also gradually come to see from God's Word and practical experience a special aspect of the subject which has brought light to some.

We have started from the beginning in Genesis 1, and there have been impressed by a simple enough fact: that the original nature of man—the human nature as we call it—came from the hands of God and consists of His own attributes, for man is made in His image. Our physical organism is a marvel and a miracle, but the image of God is to be seen peculiarly in the endowments that go to frame self-conscious personality: spirit and mind—supremely spirit, for He Himself is spirit and it is in that throne room of the personality that "spirit with Spirit can meet," and man can become a son of God; but also mind with its imagination and memory, the emotions which are the driving force of all life, and the will which makes it master of its fate. Of this masterpiece of creation it is said: "And God saw everything that He had made, and behold it was very good."

When stated thus by itself, this is commonplace. But the crux of the matter comes in the attitude we Christians take to the human personality as a consequence of the Fall. We use expressions of our own such as "total depravity," or we quote Scriptural definitions such as "dead in trespasses and sins." But how dead? In what sense totally depraved? For the Scriptures also speak of unregenerate men "who show the work of the law written in their hearts"; and that there is a light "which lighteth every man that cometh into the world"; and that all men are "His offspring" and "in Him we live and move and have our being." Does not the synthesis of these two sides of truth, and the general tenor of Scripture show us that there is only one source or upholder of life from eternity to eternity, and that all that has come from Him is perfect? Neither evil nor the devil were "in the beginning." Evil is a misuse of good. It appeared in history at an unknown date, when a being called the Lightbearer (Lucifer), "the anointed cherub," took advantage of the endowment of free will (the highest endowment in the universe, for only such can be God's fellows), and led his host in revolt against the basic law of God's nature, self-giving love, to found a new kingdom grounded in its perversion, self-seeking love. Thus Lucifer, angel of light, became Satan, prince of darkness. Good became evil. The seraph became the devil.

Adam also followed suit, but with a vastly important difference. The father of lies was the primal anti-God and anti-Christ. He rejected God and the principles of the heavenly kingdom, and substituted a rival kingdom based on the polar opposites to the nature of God—evil for good, self-love for selflessness, force for meekness, war for peace. Likewise God rejected him, and he became evil personified, with no spark of his pristine purity remaining in him, incapable of repentance, fixed in iniquity.

Adam, on the other hand, in his fall was not

a total God-rejector, a devil, but rather a world and flesh lover allured by their deceitful appeals, drawn away by his own desires and enticed. No sooner had he given consent than he was ashamed, experienced fear, and hid himself—sure evidence that all light had not died in him. And God came down, not to deliver him "into chains of darkness" but to give him the promise of a seed which would one day fructify to his redemption. It was a vastly different judgment suited to a vastly different condition.

Plainly there remained a capacity for God, a something—call it what we may—a seed, a light, a work of the law written in the heart, which is God-conscious, God-hungry, God-responsive. Do not all fishers of men sense it? The wistful acknowledgment that it must be wonderful to have a sure faith; the multitude of religions; the ready response to vital testimony in the most unlikely quarters; the search for God which neither flame nor sword nor tyrant's decree can quench? Wise soul-winners not only sense it, but give it central place in their method of approach. Jesus, the greatest of all, looked on fallen men as prodigal sons, far away but capable of return—the most tender and true of all descriptions of fallen humanity. His objective with the fallen woman at the well was to quicken and rightly direct her existing sense of thirst. He said He came to call sinners to repentance, thus affirming the existence of a spiritual ear by which sinners can hear—a sense of hearing which must consist of the same spiritual substance as the summons heard, for like can unite only with like. The eye and the thing seen are of the same substance, likewise the ear and the thing heard.

> The ear is self-same with the music,
> Beam with vision, eye with sun.

The something of God in a sinner unites, if he consents, to the calling, saving voice of the Savior come to seek him, and from that union is born the Christ within.

Then what happens? We are now coming to the point which interests us as God's children. Does the Scripture teach that a new divine nature from without is implanted in the redeemed child of God, as some separate endowment engrafted by some means in the believer? We think not. The Scripture speaks of a self, an ego, a nature, which was sin-bound, but now after passing through a death and resurrection in Christ, is sanctified and meet for the Master's use. Romans 7 says "*I* am carnal, sold under sin." Romans 6 says "Reckon ye *yourselves* to be dead indeed unto sin and alive unto God in our Lord Jesus Christ"; and "Yield *yourselves* unto God, as those that are alive from the dead." Your members were once "instruments of unrighteousness unto sin," but now "your bodies are the temples of the Holy Ghost."

What then is the self and the members, which were the property of Satan but are now the holy habitation of God? The whole man, the self, the I is the personality, the God-created mental, emotional, volitional life referred to previously. The members or body are, of course, the equally God-created physical organism. This is all now to be "alive unto God." In other words, we have not to fall into the error of regarding any created thing, not a single attribute of our nature, as bad in its origin ("I know and am persuaded of the Lord Jesus that there is nothing unclean of itself"); but merely that it has been put to evil use. Satan originated nothing, but was merely the misdirector, misuser, usurper of a nature whose endowments and capacities were originally created to manifest the glory of God.

Redemption, therefore, regains for God, through the cleansing blood and sanctifying Spirit, the full use of the human personality. "Alive unto God" means that at last poor enslaved man becomes really alive, abundantly alive—not suppressed, not maimed, not dead nor numbed, but wholly liberated. Not a life of don'ts, but of do's to the uttermost. "In whose service is perfect freedom." The Fall had defiled and cramped and clamped down man's capacities to the narrow circle of his gross and corrupted self-interest. Salvation restores them to the endless developing stimulus of the creative Spirit of God, for cooperation with whom man had been originally endowed with God-like capacities for God-like and universal productiveness. It will take all eternity to manifest forth the potentialities of human personality in cooperative submission to the Spirit of God. The whole creation waiteth for the manifestation of the sons of God.

Away, then, with the false bondage and even resentment that cripples some through the mistaken idea that there are capacities of the physical, mental or emotional life of which we should be well rid, or with which it is a puzzle to know why we were ever endowed. Every capacity is God-given, but devil-infected and earth-bound, until rescued, redeemed, restored to express forth the glories and powers of the world to come. Psychologists have seen this in dim fashion, and emphasized it in their talk of sublimation—however, with few exceptions, they can merely point to the ideal "sublimation," but know not the "master sentiment" of love to Christ by which alone it can be realized in entirety.

Full Manhood Realized

A remaining matter of importance is the way by which this liberated, resurrected life in Christ can be ours in experience. Many different interpretations of Scripture are given on this point. Some emphasize that as the believer is born of the Spirit, so in logical sequence He will grow in the Spirit, so long as he recognizes the responsibility upon him to cooperate by faith and works. Others, using the type of the crossing of Jordan following upon the passage of the Red Sea (as expounded, for instance, in Hebrews 4), or such New Testament examples as Pentecost and the coming of the Spirit upon the believers of Samaria, teach the necessity of a second definite crisis of sanctification, and date the vigorous growth of the believer in the ways of God only as subsequent to this second work of grace. Some go even farther and teach that the filling of the Spirit, to be genuine, must be accompanied by outward signs, as in some instances in the book of the Acts. The great saints of past centuries used to speak of the way into the deeps of God as the *via negativa,* the highway of purgation, illumination and union through which all purified souls must pass to reach the full fruition of the eternal embrace.

We can only give truth as we see it from the Scriptures, and on a thorny question such as this we must make it clear that it is only the personal viewpoint of the writer, for the WEC gives full latitude within its ranks for all variations of conviction on these lesser points. To us it seems clear that all Christian experience is dependent upon the sole condition "according to your faith be it unto you," and that, beyond this no single method of realizing the Spirit-filled life is revealed. An outline of truth is given, especially in the basic epistle to the Romans, expounding the full implications of the process of Christ in His incarnation, life, death, resurrection, ascen-

sion and return. Justification is there set forth
(Rom. 3), then sanctification (Rom. 6), then
the triumphing life, the guided life, the fruitful
life, the empowered life, the sacrificial life, and
so on (Rom. 8).

It does not seem to us that the exact way of
realization is delineated in the form of special
crises, but rather that the table is spread, and
then we are told that faith helps itself. But it
does insist that the evidence of true life in God
is that we do help ourselves and go from grace
to grace and from strength to strength. We are
justified; well, are we sanctified? Do we have a
vital experience of Christ's death and resurrection inwrought in us as outlined in Romans 6,
as well as merely appropriated by us in a vicari-
ous and outward sense for sins forgiven? Are we
only vaguely "reckoning" ourselves as dead and
risen with Him, with an underlying unbelief
that it really is so? Or is it an actual inwrought
experience?

Being human, we can only receive infinite
truth in finite doses, eternal indivisible realities
in apparently divisible sections suited to our
temporal outlook. Thus, for instance, most of us
see our need of justification and then only later

of sanctification. Actually, all has been given us eternally and completely in Christ; and this is the truth emphasized by those who stress gradual growth. But, because we are human and finite, for very many of us (but not necessarily for all) Christian experience is more like the scaling of a flight of steps than progress along a smooth road. As we see a new step of advance, we take it. After justification, it gradually dawns on us that we have an inward enemy, the flesh, to be dealt with, as well as the outward defilement of our gross sins which were blotted out on our first approach to Calvary. We find ourselves still in bondage to inward corruption, producing outward falls, and with a vastly greater self-consciousness than God-consciousness interfering with outward witness and inward peace. We cry with the apostle, "I am carnal, sold under sin."

Actually we are not so from the Godward aspect, for we are sanctified once and for all in Christ, but faith has so far failed to possess all its possessions: we still live under a delusion through unbelief—that we are carnal, when we are not carnal in Christ; and unbelief is as potent in its realm as faith, for it is merely a reversed form of faith, belief in the power of evil in place of belief in the power of God. Thus in actual experience we feel and see carnality, until unbelief is reversed and transmuted into bold acceptance and declaration of the established truth in Christ, that we *are* dead and that our life *is* hid with Him in God. This is for many of us a second experience; and again we stress that it must be the actual experience of all of us who would go on with God, whether we call it second or no.

It has been, as said above, a further stage in the appropriation of faith, a fulfillment of the one law of the new life "according to your faith be it unto you." And, do not let us forget, faith begins by being a labor (Heb. 6:11–12) or fight (1 Tim. 6:12), although it is consummated in a rest (Heb. 4:3). That is to say, the first stage of faith is always the battle of taking hold by the will, heart, and intelligence of some truth or promise which is not real to us in experience, and declaring it to be ours in spite of appearances. We do not appear to be dead unto sin and alive unto God. We are told to believe it, and so we dare to do so and declare so. A thousand times, maybe, faith will be assaulted and fall: unbelief will say "nonsense," and we shall belie our declaration of faith. But the fight or labor of faith means that we deliberately return to the assault. Once again we believe and declare it. This we persist in doing. As we thus follow in the steps of those who "by faith and patience" inherit the promises, a new divine thing will happen within us. The Spirit will cooperate with our faith (as He is invisibly doing all the time), and to faith will be added assurance. Labor and fight will be replaced by rest. The consummation of faith has been reached. What was once an effort to attain or maintain, now becomes as natural as breathing. Such is the law of faith, whether exercised in sanctification or in any of the later and higher reaches of Christian experience.

To sum up, our God-given human nature is a dynamic potential, which can be directed, according to the aims of its chosen overlord, to good or evil. In the Fall it has been "sold under sin," but now in the redemption that is in Christ Jesus, "we" (our original selves) are bought back from the usurper, and bidden to reckon ourselves "alive unto God" and to "yield yourselves unto God as those that are alive from the dead."

The root of this release is found in the substitutionary death of Christ and our realization of our identification with Him in the cross. This does not mean that some part of us is to die, but that we are to see ourselves in Christ as those who have passed through an experience of death so far as any further acknowledgment of the lordship of Satan and union with sin are concerned. Nothing in us ourselves has died. There is no such thing as the death of self or death to self. Rather, God now reunites us to Himself for the purpose of expressing His own glory through our "selves." We have passed on beyond the cross, out of the tomb into the resurrection. The emotions now express love for God and man, hatred of evil, jealousy for God's glory, pride (glory) in the cross. The imagination and intuition are vibrant with a constant sight and sense of Him whom having not seen we love, and with a vision of His love for the world. The will makes choices and declarations of faith. The body uses its capacities both in sounding forth His praise and sharing in the preaching of the gospel to every creature. The same self, the same "I," but now the willing servant and son of the Spirit.

Thus, in a word, we have seen the way of the Spirit to be transmutation: the losing of nothing with which God has endowed us, but the transmuting of the whole self from a fleshly to a spiritual kingdom. This fact has meant to us a new and exhilarating freedom, a knowledge that in Christ we have come to full manhood and womanhood, with every endowment of the human nature "holy unto the Lord."

10

The Law of Spiritual Harvest

FINALLY, for what are we emancipated? What is the consummation of discipleship in this life? What of the Master, the Pattern? "I came that *they* might have life." "He saved *others,* Himself He could not save." "The Son of man came . . . to give His life a ransom for *many.*" With sure instinct all Christianity has chosen for its symbol the cross, for the principle which it objectified in history is woven into the very texture of the nature of God. There was the cross at the dawn of history when "the Lamb was slain from the foundation of the world." There was the cross when "though He was rich, yet for your sakes He became poor." There was the cross at the manger. It was there when He left His earthly home; on the mount of temptation; throughout the three years when "the Son of man had not where to lay His head." This all was the way of the cross; and the mystery of that way, the secret revealed to the initiates of the Spirit, is both the Alpha and Omega of the disciple's way of life on earth.

This "way of the cross" has three aspects. The first we all know. As sinners, we see and receive Christ crucified as our substitute. Another went to the cross for us and in our stead, and His dying for us in infinite mercy and grace expiated the consequences of the broken law, and gained for us forgiveness, cleansing from guilt, justification and regeneration.

The second many know. It is clearly expounded in Scripture and realized in the experience of all who go on with God. It is commonly called identification with Christ's cross. The Christian sees that not only has he come *to* the cross, but is himself *on* it. For if Christ died in my place, then in the sight of God it was I that died. "I am crucified with Christ" sums up in a sentence Paul's many references to this vital truth. When to knowledge is added eager appropriation, then the dying of the "old man" and rising of the "new man" in Christ becomes a permanent inward experience in the personality, to which the outward life, as always, is conformed.

But upon the third and final stage in this upward, rugged track to the summit of being, only the few, Christ's very brethren, make a vigorous ascent. It is the way of the cross for world redemption. It is the law of the spiritual harvest. The two former aspects of the cross are for my own benefit; this third is for others. Supremely is it seen in Christ. For others He went forth from His baptism and anointing to walk this way. For others He died daily to loved ones, home and the normal enjoyments of living. For others He laid down His life. And this He did to fulfill the law of spiritual harvest. It was a necessity. Fallen man had died in the spirit to God and the kingdom of heaven, and come alive in the flesh to Satan and the kingdom of hell. A Savior and Pioneer (Heb. 2:10) must be found, who could and would die to the kingdom of hell as fallen man's substitute, rise again to the kingdom of heaven for him, and thus become the seed-corn which by its death produces the hundredfold of life-giving sustenance, not for itself, but for those who feed on it. With this "joy set before Him"—the joy of the harvest, the joy of the mother who travails to give birth—"He endured the Cross, despising the shame" (Heb. 12:2).

In His footsteps followed the first members of His Church. They saw the full stature of Christian living to consist, not merely in the enjoyment of the fruits of Christ's passion, but in the sharing of the passion itself for the saving of others. "So death worketh in us, but life in you," wrote Paul; and "I now rejoice in my sufferings for you, and fill up that which is behind of the afflictions of Christ in my flesh for His body's sake."

Here is a final fact of vast practical importance and a door of unending opportunity. If I am Christ's, then voluntary "deaths" to the normal advantages in the flesh, comforts, loved ones, material advancement, enlarged income, pleasures, leisure, give me the right to claim and receive the harvest in the Spirit. Instead of regarding such as losses and deprivations to be endured if necessary but avoided if possible, we deliberately embrace them and glory in them as the way of the harvest. Equally we turn all life's unsought "trials" to the same use: tragedies, injustices, slights, insults, losses. As a matter of fact, although unsought, none are unsuited. Each comes because it just fits our case, and each is resisted as an impudent gatecrasher or welcomed as friend and ally with corresponding destructive or constructive effect. "Awake, O north wind; blow upon my garden, that the spices thereof may flow out." By the practice of this principle of the cross, losses and trials, whether unsought or deliberately chosen, become positive weapons of offense in destroying the works of the devil and loosening his grip on humanity—even as Christ's death, thus embraced, destroyed him who had the power of death and led captivity captive.

I know no man who understood this better than C.T. Studd, the founder of this crusade. In the evening of their lives, the call came to him to pioneer work in Africa, where Mrs. Studd, at that time an invalid, could not accompany him. Both realized that the call could only be fulfilled by a broken home and maybe years of separation, and both accepted it, only because they understood this law of the harvest, "death in us . . . life in others." From that "way of the cross" entered upon in 1913, and endured unflinchingly till their long separation ended in their glorification in 1931 and 1928 respectively, has sprung this great and growing work with its harvest of changed lives already being reaped in Congo, and fresh crops showing well above ground in a dozen other lands.

This book was produced by CLC Publications. We hope it has been life-changing and has given you a fresh experience of God through the work of the Holy Spirit. CLC Publications is an outreach of CLC Ministries International, a global literature mission with work in over fifty countries. If you would like to know more about us or are interested in opportunities to serve with a faith mission, we invite you to contact us at:

CLC Ministries International
PO Box 1449
Fort Washington, PA 19034

E-mail: mail@clcusa.org
Website: www.clcpublications.com

DO YOU LOVE GOOD CHRISTIAN BOOKS?
Do you have a heart for worldwide missions?

You can receive a FREE subscription to CLC's newsletter on global literature missions

Order by e-mail at:

clcworld@clcusa.org

or mail your request to:

**PO Box 1449
Fort Washington, PA 19034**